The Big Book of
Random Facts

1000 Interesting Facts and Trivia

Interesting Trivia
and Funny Facts Vol.2

Bill O´Neill

Disclaimer

This book contains interesting facts and trivia about things you didn't know and likely don't care about, but it's fun! These trivia facts are perfect for playing pub quizzes with your friends or just a night in with random facts you didn't know about. Funny facts go a long way. Enjoy the read!

As of February 22nd 2017, this book has been edited to provide better quality and value.

1. The beer Pabst Blue Ribbon, known more casually PBR, was made famous at the 1893 World's Fair in Chicago, Illinois. It received its iconic name because it won the blue ribbon for best beer.

2. The United States of America contains five separate states with no sales tax: New Hampshire, Oregon, Montana, Delaware, and Alaska.

3. Penguins and Kiwis, although from radically different ecosystems, are both flightless birds.

4. Australia is geographically larger than the United States of America, and is also the world's largest island.

5. The Stolen Generation refers to aboriginal Australian children who were forcibly removed from their families by local governing bodies.

6. The Warped Tour first occurred in the summer of 1995. It became the Vans Warped Tour in 1996.

7. The popular reality television show Project Runway has aired 14 seasons, spawned 5

spinoff shows, and inspired numerous international versions of the show.

8.   Tonic water was once a common medicine for preventing malaria.

9.   America's Historic Route 66 stretched from the California coast to Chicago, Illinois. It was also known as "The Mother Road."

10. The Ivy League collection of Universities includes: Brown, Columbia, Cornell, Dartmouth, Harvard, University of Pennsylvania, Princeton, and Yale.

11. Singer and songwriter Elliott Smith was born in Omaha, Nebraska.

12. The only living member of the *Ailuridae* family is the red panda.

13. Google's unofficial slogan until 2015 was "don't be evil."

14. The Disney Channel first began airing content in 1983. Its first program was a show called *Good Morning, Mickey!*

15. Daria Morgendorffer, from the MTV2 animated show *Daria*, was originally a character

from a different successful MTV animated series, *Beavis and Butt-Head*.

16. The first iPhone was released for sale in 2007.

17. Uppercase and lowercase are terms based in antiquated forms of text printing. When printmakers used to create words by putting together individual letters, capitalized letters were kept and organized in an upper case, while uncapitalized letters were kept in a lower case, for ease of use.

18. The average lifespan of a goldfish, depending on its environment and caretaking, can range from a few months to as much as 25 years!

19. The city Corpus Christi, located in Texas, literally translates as "body of Christ" from Latin to English.

20. The official languages of the Republic of Madagascar are Malagasy and French.

21. *Song of the South* (1946), Walt Disney's first movie to incorporate live actors alongside its animated characters, has never been fully released on home video in the United States.

22. Before it became known as Silicon Valley, the region of northern California home to America's densest concentration of technology companies and startups was known as "The Valley of Hearts Delight."

23. A microbrewery is defined as creating no more than 15,000 barrels of beer each year. They are also independently owned.

24. Hello Kitty, the most famous character in the Sanrio roster, has a net worth of $5 billion USD.

25. Before starring in the popular *Star Trek* series, Chris Pine's first full-feature film role was in *The Princess Diaries II: Royal Engagement* in 2003.

26. The first bicycle was created in Germany in 1817. It was called a laufmaschine in German.

27. Mount Everest is the highest mountain point in the world, measuring at 29,029 feet.

28. In 2013, The National Football League (NFL) penned a deal with the lingerie brand PINK, an entity of Victoria's Secret, in order to increase exposure to teenage girls and college-age women.

29. It is a myth that owls can complete a full 360-degree rotation with their heads. They can, however, turn approximately 200 degrees.

30. The official Chicago flag features four stars in its design, each one symbolizing a major event in the city's history: Fort Dearborn, the Great Chicago Fire, The World's Columbian Exposition, and the Century of Progress Exposition.

31. Utah is nicknamed 'The Beehive State' as a tribute to its core values of efficiency, industry, and hard work. The state route symbol is a beehive as well.

32. Dr. Seuss, born Theodor Seuss Geisel, published almost 70 children's books during his career.

33. Barbie, the iconic fashion doll by Mattel, Inc., was named after the designer's own daughter, Barbara.

34. Falling vending machines cause an average of 2.18 deaths annually.

35. Before becoming a famous drag queen, RuPaul was in a punk band called Wee Wee Pole.

36. A sun dog is a visual phenomenon in which a halo of light appears to surround the sun.

37. Tom Brady, quarterback for the NFL New England Patriots, was a 6th-round pick in the 2000 draft.

38. Old and discarded tires can be ground into rubber crumb and used as fill for artificial turf fields.

39. Oliver and James Phelps, who played the Weasley twins in the Harry Potter movie series, naturally have brown hair, not red hair.

40. Over 150 species of roses exist in the world.

41. House centipedes can have as many as 15 legs. They also eat other insects, including cockroaches and spiders.

42. The largest known collection of Beanie Babies totals at 20,000 toys. The most valuable Beanie Baby is Princess, designed in memoriam of the late Princess Diana.

43. The "&" symbol is formally known as an ampersand.

44. There are over 500 shades of gray visible to the human eye.

45. Umami is one the five basic taste categories, best translated as 'savory.'

46. Jellyfish both eat and discard waste through a single opening, or mouth, in their body.

47. In 2016, the top grossing box office star was Harrison Ford. The top grossing female box office star was Scarlett Johansson and, in comparison, is 10th in the overall ranking.

48. David Ortiz, the designated hitter for the MLB team the Boston Red Sox, has hit an impressive 497 career home runs.

49. The United States Air Force trains 10 people every year in Morse Code communications.

50. Slugs are snail-like creatures which lack a shell.

51. Your ape index is the measured ratio of your full wingspan, or arm span, relative to your height.

52. In tattoo culture, the iconic swallow was originally a sailor tattoo that symbolized a sailor's first voyage at sea.

53. Mardi Gras, as a religious holiday, is a celebration which occurs on the last day before

the fasting period of Lent. It is also nicknamed Shrove Tuesday.

54. In 1938, Babe Didrikson Zaharias was the first woman to play in the otherwise all-male Professional Golf Association (PGA) tour. She later helped to establish the Ladies Professional Golf Association (LPGA) in 1949.

55. Curriculum vitae translates literally into "the course of life."

56. Walt Disney's *Snow White and the Seven Dwarfs* was initially released in 1937, and it was their first full-length animated film.

57. Llamas spit at other llamas, and occasionally humans, as a method of asserting dominance or aggressiveness.

58. The only game in which the New York Yankees have not thrown a ceremonial first pitch to signal the beginning of a game was the home opening game in 1978.

59. Eggplant is typically categorized as a vegetable but is actually a fruit.

60. Before becoming a beloved household icon and chef, Julia Child worked for the Office of

Strategic Services (OSS), an early form of the Central Intelligence Agency (CIA).

61. Snowboarding became an official Olympic sport in 1998.

62. The Backstreet Boys are considered the most successful boy band in music history based on their record sales; they have sold over 130 million records over the span of their 16-year career.

63. Carrot flies are insects which attack carrots, parsnips, celery, and parsley.

64. Cork material, as found in wine stoppers and cork boards, is not made with the bark from cork trees.

65. Although English is the second most widely spoken language according to total number of speakers in the world, it only ranks third based on the total number of native speakers. Mandarin Chinese ranks first in both categories.

66. The iconic Apple brand logo was first designed with a rainbow color scheme to make it more

human-like and approachable. In 1999, the company transitioned into monochrome styles.

67. Capoeira is a form of martial arts with roots in acrobatics, dance, and live music, and is native to Brazil. Its origins can be traced back to the country's history of African slavery.

68. The state motto of New Hampshire in the United States of America is "Live Free or Die."

69. In Chinese culture, white symbolizes death and mourning.

70. The first tarot cards appeared in Italy in the early 1400s.

71. Johnny Cash was a neighbor to fellow well-known recording artist Roy Orbison for 20 years when they lived in Tennessee.

72. Pangea was the last supercontinent to exist on Earth and began to separate approximately 175 million years ago.

73. A serif typeface is one which contains small lines on the ends of certain letters, particularly capitalized letters. The opposite is a sans serif typeface.

74. There are five categories of Nobel Prizes: chemistry, physics, physiology and medicine, literature, and peace.

75. The average human body contains between 500 and 700 lymph nodes.

76. Director Wes Anderson and actor Owen Wilson were roommates during their time as students at the University of Texas at Austin. Wilson has since appeared in some form in almost every movie Anderson has created.

77. Paan, a traditional Indian snack, is made from betel leaf and nuts, which are proven psychoactive substances.

78. The top earning YouTube personality of 2015, PewDiePie, earned $12 million dollars that year.

79. A human sneeze can travel as far as 200 feet away from its starting point.

80. The national currency of the Republic of Serbia is the Dinar.

81. The entire land area of Hawaii measures 16,635 km². In comparison, Connecticut only measures 12,541 km².

82. Martin Scorsese is 5 feet and 4 inches tall.

83. The anime film *My Neighbor Totoro* was partially biographic and based on director Hayao Miyazaki's own childhood.

84. Seals and sea lions are both pinnipeds, meaning that they are semi-aquatic mammals.

85. The voice actor of the beloved 1977 Disney animated film *The Many Adventures of Winnie The Pooh*, Sterling Holloway, appeared in several other Disney animated films. Among his most well-known performances are his roles as the Cheshire Cat in *Alice In Wonderland*, Kaa the snake in *The Jungle Book*, and Roquefort the mouse in *The Aristocats*.

86. The official logo for the NFL team the Seattle Seahawks was inspired by a Native American Kwakwaka'waw wooden mask.

87. Jean Shepard, author and autobiographer of *In God We Trust, All Others Pay In Cash*, makes a cameo in his own story in the 1983 film *A Christmas Story*. In the film, he plays an adult who tells off his childhood self.

88. Humans are born with 270 bones in their body, but with age this number decreases to 206.

89. Red velvet mites earned their name thanks to their vibrant color and soft-looking texture. Despite their name, they are classified as arachnids.

90. The first masking tape was invented in 1922.

91. Throughout the state of Maine, it is against the law to keep your Christmas decorations up past January 14th. If you do, you will be fined.

92. There are currently 722 revealed Pokémon monster species across all the franchise's platforms and storylines.

93. Baby porcupines are called porcupettes and are born with soft quills which harden with age. They are unrelated to hedgehogs.

94. John Wilkes Booth's first career was as an actor.

95. Kool-Aid was invented in 1927 in Hastings, Nebraska.

96. J.K. Rowling's series *Harry Potter* has been translated into 74 different languages.

97. The Trans-Siberian Railway is the longest railway in the world, measuring 9,289 km.

98. Steve Jobs took over Pixar in 1986. When Disney purchased the animation company in 2006, Jobs became Disney's single largest shareholder.

99. Lacrosse was first played by eastern Woodland Native Americans and some Plains Indian tribes as early as the 17th century.

100. Canadian actor Seth Rogan's first full-feature film appearance was in the 2001 cult classic *Donnie Darko*.

101. There is an event called the Mermaid Parade which occurs annually in Coney Island, New York. This parade celebrates the official beginning of the summer season.

102. Alpacas were initially bred solely for their fibers.

103. Hillary Rodham Clinton was the president of the Wellesley Young Republican's Club during her first year of undergraduate studies at Wellesley College.

104. The number 2 is the only even prime number.

105. The young contestants in the final beauty pageant scene in *Little Miss Sunshine* were all real beauty pageant competitors.

106. The aurora australis, otherwise known as the southern lights, is the counterpart phenomenon to the aurora borealis, which is known as the northern lights.

107. A normal National Hockey League (NHL) game will use an average of 12 hockey pucks.

108. The world's largest IKEA retail store is located in Stockholm, Sweden. It measures 594,000 ft^2.

109. The Republic of Niger abolished slavery in 1960. However, it was still legal until 2003.

110. In the popular *Scooby Doo* franchise, Shaggy's full name is Norville Rogers. Scooby's full name is Scoobert.

111. The most recent iteration of the Times Square New Year's Eve Ball is composed of over 32,000 LED lamps.

112. Michael Bloomberg's birthday is the same day as Valentine's Day.

113. The Shakers, otherwise known as the Shaking Quakers, are a sect of Christianity derived from the Quakers. They received their name because of their ecstatic, excited worship practices.

114. Alcatraz Federal Penitentiary housed some of the most famous criminals of the early 20th century, including Al Capone, Alvin "Creepy" Karpis, George "Machine Gun" Kelly, and Robert "The Birdman Of Alcatraz" Stroud.

115. The koala is one of three mammals which can survive on a diet of only eucalyptus.

116. Watermelon is both a fruit and a vegetable. Additionally, the rind is edible.

117. The infamous typeface Comic Sans was first created in 1994 for the short-lived software program Microsoft Bob. It became widely recognized after its implementation in the early releases of Microsoft Movie Maker.

118. The Ninkasi Brewing Company's name is inspired by the Sumerian patron goddess of brewing and alcohol.

119. Chihuahua dogs are named after the state in Mexico in which their ancestors were originally bred.

120. Kaitlin Olson and Rob McElhenney, who play Sweet Dee and Mac on the popular TV comedy series *It's Always Sunny in Philadelphia*, were married in real life in 2008.

121. The name for the fifth day of the week, Thursday, was originally inspired by the Norse god Thor.

122. The recognized regional language of Portugal is Mirandese.

123. Every year, approximately 10 million cars are recycled.

124. Christ the Redeemer, the iconic statue in Rio de Janeiro, Brazil, measures 124 feet tall from foundation to peak. In comparison, the Statue of Liberty measures 151 feet tall from ground to the tip of the torch.

125. In the Cartoon Network animated series *Dexter's Laboratory*, the title character is 8 years old.

126. Lego were invented by a Danish woodworker named Ole Kirk Kristiansen in 1932. The brand's name is a portmanteau of the Danish phrase "leg godt," which translate in English as "play well."

127. The online and mobile video game Candy Crush makes approximately $633,000 daily.

128. Betsey Johnson was the head cheerleader at Syracuse University before becoming a quirky, well-known fashion designer.

129. The first patent for the ballpoint pen dates to 1888 and was awarded to John J. Loud.

130. Quentin Tarantino's first film was a short comedy piece titled *My Best Friend's Birthday*.

131. The first signs of the dovetail joint design, known for its remarkable tensile strength and durability, can be traced back to Ancient Egyptian and Chinese tombs.

132. Tennis stars and sisters Venus and Serena Williams have played eight Grand Slam finals against one another. Between them both, they have accumulated 29 Grand Slam singles titles.

133. Americans drink, on average, 400 million cups of coffee every day.

134. The washboard was invented in 1797 in New Hampshire by Nathaniel Briggs.

135. Tina Fey got her start in comedy with Second City comedy troupe in Chicago, Illinois. Other notable alumni include Steve Carell, Amy Pohler, the late Chris Farley, Stephen Colbert, and Alan Arkin.

136. Cooper Manning, the elder brother to football stars Peyton and Eli Manning, also works in the professional sports industry, but not as a player. He is host of Fox Sports' "The Manning Hour" program.

137. The number of dimples on a standard golf ball ranges from 300 to 500 on average.

138. The Brazilian wandering spider is considered the deadliest spider known to man. It has an average leg span of 13 to 15 centimeters.

139. Rummikub is a tile-based game which incorporates elements of the classic Chinese tile-based game mahjong and the card game rummy. Its origins are in Romania.

140. Black pepper is a flowering vine. It is sold as a spice after the subsequent fruit is dried and ground, but is also sold in peppercorn form as well.

141. Glass fire grenades were an early form of fire extinguishers made from 1870 to 1910. They were meant to be thrown into the fire to release the chemicals inside.

142. USB is the commonly used acronym for universal serial bus.

143. National Garlic Day is April 19th.

144. The Claymation characters Gumby's horse and dog are named Pokey and Nopey, respectively.

145. The graham cracker was first created by Sylvester Graham, a Presbyterian minister, as a means for eradicating sinful sexual desires.

146. There are 24 recognized time zones on Earth.

147. The first Walmart opened in Rogers, Arkansas.

148. Black rights activist Malcolm X was one-fourth white.

149. Singer-songwriter Vanessa Carlton wrote her breakout hit "A Thousand Miles" about the passing of her grandfather.

150. The world record for number of skips when stone skipping is 88.

151. Both Ben Cohen and Jerry Greenfield, founders of the ice cream brand Ben & Jerry's, are still alive.

152. British comedy troupe Monty Python first aired on television on October 5, 1969, through BBC Broadcasting.

153. In 2011, Netflix tested a program called Qwikster which separated their DVD rental and streaming services. It only lasted 1 month.

154. Author Kurt Vonnegut's most well-known work is his novel *Slaughterhouse Five*.

155. The Internal Revenue Service (IRS) in the United States was formed in 1862.

156. The earliest variations of sunglasses were worn by Inuit people. They were made of walrus ivory and were shaped as flat discs with thin slits cut across them to allow the wearer to see.

157. The first birth control clinic in the United States was located in Brooklyn, New York.

158. Zebras are black with white stripes.

159. The thinnest laptop currently on the market measures 10.4 mm, or .41 inches, thin.

160. The first self-healing elastomer was invented in 2007. It was made with silicone rubber.

161. A human foot can produce over .25 US pints of sweat every day.

162. Balsamic vinegar does not contain any actual balsam.

163. Tommy Wiseau was the director, writer, and protagonist in his 2003 cult classic *The Room*.

164. Women's button-up shirts are designed with the buttons opposite of men's shirts based on Victorian styles in which women were dressed by servants, thus orienting the buttons for the dresser.

165. The *Star Trek* television series created 726 episodes over 30 seasons.

166. Contemporary gothic fashion is inspired by the Victorian Era mourning style of dress.

167. Tug of War was an official sport in the summer Olympics from 1900 to 1920.

168. The first painting Jackson Pollock sold to a museum was his work *The She-Wolf*. It was purchased by the Museum of Modern Art (MoMA) in 1944 for $650.

169. In Nara Park in Japan is famous for its sika deer, which roam freely and politely through the park.

170. Dr. Martens boots were designed by a World War II German army doctor named Kaus Märtens.

171. Operation Desert Farewell was the movement by the United States during the Gulf War conflict to return its units and equipment back to the US.

172. The Japanese language has a consonant-vowel structure.

173. Halloween is rooted in an ancient Celtic holiday called Samhain, which marked the beginning of their new year.

174. An alternative name for a Moscow Mule cocktail is a Vodka Buck.

175. The longest baseball game in history lasted 33 innings, with a running time of eight hours and twenty-five minutes of play.

176. Emoticons are text-based versions of facial expressions. In contrast, emojis are pictographs.

177. Wisconsin, Wyoming, is the largest producer of cheese in the United States.

178. It is a myth that it takes fewer facial muscles to smile than to frown.

179. The ester butyl acetate is found in both nail polish and bananas.

180. Angkor Wat, the ancient temple grounds in Cambodia, is the largest religious monument in the world.

181. Step pyramids were the primary design choice in Mesoamerican pyramid architecture, most notably constructed by the Aztecs and Mayans.

182. The Joshua Tree plant is almost exclusively found in the Mojave Desert.

183. Whiskey poker is an old form of poker in which players only draw from the communal hand in the center of the table.

184. Chti is a dialect of French spoken in the far North regions of the country. It is formally known as Picard.

185. After the 14th Dalai Lama fled to India from Tibet in 1959 during the Chinese invasion, approximately 80,000 Tibetans followed him to re-settle.

186. Jellygraph is a method of printing where an image is prepared with special inks and then transferred to a gelatin-based surface.

187. Genuphobia is the fear of knees.

188. A roller derby team has five players on the track during play.

189. Rapper Kanye West's father, Ray West, was a former member of the Black Panthers.

190. Coca-Cola's first formulation was an alcoholic drink called Pemberton's French Wine Coca nerve tonic. The non-alcoholic version was created in response to prohibition.

191. Johnny Rotten, lead singer of the Sex Pistols, was born John Joseph Lydon.

192. The adult animated series *South Park* has been nominated for an Emmy Award 16 times and has won 4 times.

193. Fascia is the connective tissue in the human body which lies between skin and muscles.

194. Olympic swimmer Michael Phelps has hypermobile ankles.

195. In the popular anime series *Sailor Moon*, characters Uranus and Neptune are portrayed as cousins in the English dubbed translation. In the original Japanese, they are written as lovers.

196. The National Aeronautics and Space Administration (NASA) has a service which allows them to send you a text or email message every time the International Space Station passes overhead.

197. Eddie Aikau, the first lifeguard to ever monitor Waimea Bay on Oahu, Hawaii, saved over 500 people during his work.

198. The first spokesperson for MAC Cosmetics Viva Glam campaign was drag queen RuPaul in 1994.

199. The US Army debuted its own digital camouflage print in 2004, labeled the Universal Camouflage Pattern.

200. Moose, caribou, and elk are all members of the deer family.

201. Balsa wood is one of the primary materials used in making table tennis paddles.

202. The annual Steampunk World's Fair is held in Piscataway, New Jersey.

203. Singer Whitney Houston was one of the producers behind the original *Princess Diaries* film.

204. Tiki torches first became popular in the United States in the 1930s.

205. Stained glass was a method of depicting the narratives of the Bible for the illiterate masses during the Middle Ages.

206. Before being adopted as the symbol of the Nazi Party, the swastika was, and still is, a religious symbol in Indian religions such as Hinduism and Buddhism.

207. The original Teddy bear was named after former president Theodore "Teddy" Roosevelt.

208. Baseball legend Babe Ruth's first team was the Baltimore Orioles.

209. Charles M. Shultz wrote 17,897 *Peanuts* comic strips before his passing.

210. Floppy disks were available in three main sizes, 20cm, 13cm, and 9cm.

211. South Carolina has the largest percentage of mobile home housing units in the United States at 18.8%.

212. Not all palm trees are trees. They can also appear as shrubs or vines.

213. Prince Edward Island is the only province of Canada with no land boundary.

214. AM radio, or amplitude modulation radio, was the first type of audio radio transmission.

215. The late boxer Muhammad Ali was born Cassius Marcellus Clay.

216. "Georgia On My Mind," made famous by the late recording artist Ray Charles, is the official song of the state of Georgia.

217. The name for the IQ society Mensa International is not an acronym. It is derived from the Latin word *mensa*, meaning table, symbolizing the importance of equality and cooperation in the organization.

218. The first state to register automobiles in the United States was New York.

219. The last immigrant to pass through inspection at Ellis Island was in 1954.

220. The Akan are the dominant ethnic group residing in the Republic of Côte d'Ivoire.

221. The typeface used on road signs throughout the United Kingdom is called Transport.

222. Characters Mario, Luigi, and Wario in the *Super Mario* franchise have all been voiced by the same voice actor, Charles Martinet, since 1995.

223. LIFE magazine ran as a weekly publication from 1883 to 1972.

224. The top 13 golfers with the most PGA tour wins are all from the United States.

225. Greece became a member of the Eurozone in 2000.

226. It is illegal to wear a thong bikini in public in Melbourne, Florida.

227. Ryan Sheckler was 13 years old when he won his first gold medal at the summer X Games in 2003, making him the youngest ever gold medalist in the games' history.

228. The Vera Bradley brand got its start in Fort Wayne, Indiana.

229. Sappho is an ancient Greek poetess referred to in artifacts as the Tenth muse.

230. Recording artist Justin Timberlake became a co-owner of the social media website Myspace in 2011.

231. David Bowie, born David Robert Jones, was born in Brixton, London, England.

232. Jacqueline "Jackie" Kennedy became a member of the International Best Dressed List Hall of Fame in 1965.

233. The city Portland, Oregon, was named after the city Portland, Maine.

234. The MLB team Los Angeles Angels of Anaheim have had four different names since becoming a team in 1961.

235. There are nine active teams and six former teams in the Major League Lacrosse league.

236. An average of 205,400 passengers arrive and depart through Heathrow International Airport every day.

237. The resulting offspring of a sheep and a goat is known as a geep in popular media.

238. Emu chicks are nurtured by the father rather than the mother.

239. The Haunted Mansion ride at the various Disney franchise theme parks calls its cars 'Doombuggies'.

240. Rosa Parks was the secretary of her Montgomery, Alabama, chapter of the NAACP before her famous bus boycott in 1955.

241. Bodybuilding as a sport was banned in China in 1953. This ban was removed 30 years later.

242. Approximately 54% of working adults in the Kingdom of Belgium belong to a union.

243. The cyberpunk genre, and subsequent derivatives including steampunk, solarpunk, and decopunk, are all rooted in retrofuturism.

244. *The Jetsons* was set in the year 2062.

245. Matt Damon worked with real NASA astronauts while filming *The Martian* in order to maintain the authenticity of the movie.

246. Soccer, or association football, is the most popular sport in the world, with over 250 million players.

247. The protein keratin is found both in human fingernails and animal claws.

248. Canadian actor Dan Aykroyd has webbed feet.

249. The most expensive piano in the world is made of transparent materials and is called the Crystal Piano. It sold for $3.22 million USD.

250. A cheetah can accelerate from 0 to 60 miles per hour in 3 seconds.

251. Comic-Con International, which hosts the well-known annual San Diego Comic-Con convention, is a non-profit organization.

252. The original title for the FX animated series *Archer* was *Duchess*. Duchess, in the series, is the protagonist Sterling Archer's codename.

253. The events for the women's heptathlon competition, in order, are the 100 meter hurdle, shotput, high jump, 200 meter run, long jump, javelin throw, and an 800 meter run.

254. Israel's bank notes, known as the Israeli new shekel, are printed with Braille on them.

255. George Clooney was one of nine actors to play the role of Batman in the various Hollywood film adaptations.

256. British spy novelist John Le Carre's real name is David Cornewell. He published under the name Le Carre because while he was working as a member of the British Foreign Office, he could not publish work under his own name.

257. Men's Olympic Gymnasts compete in six events, while women compete in four.

258. The iconic America Online (AOL) running man symbol was inspired by American postwar branding images in the 1940's and 1950's.

259. The official mascot for the 1976 Innsbruck Winter Olympics, the first ever Winter games, was a snowman named Schneemann.

260. The Great Mississippi Flood of 1927, documented as the most destructive river flood in United States history, is known as the Good Friday Flood by residents at the time.

261. The phrase "tying the knot" is inspired by the classic pretzel knot shape. In Swiss culture, it is a tradition for newlyweds to make a wish and break a pretzel together.

262. A sunflower will have either 34, 55, or 89 petals depending on is size.

263. The predecessor to the card game bridge is called Russian Whist.

264. In 1818, Sir WIlliam Cubitt invented the treadmill as a form of punishment for prisoners.

265. There are 33,500 public school district borders in the United States.

266. Male geisha are known as taikomochi or hōkan.

267. Humans can literally not be "double jointed." This term refers to hypermobility in various parts of the body.

268. Narwhals are most closely related to the beluga whale.

269. Sliced bread was first marketed and sold in the United States in 1928.

270. Morocco, France, and Spain are the only countries to have both Mediterranean and Atlantic coastlines.

271. The longest recorded period of a person going without sleep is 264 hours, approximately 11 days.

272. The first set of crayons, created by Crayola, was made in 1903 and cost five cents.

273. The fennec fox is the smallest in its species.

274. It is illegal to possess or distribute pornography in Botswana.

275. The highest mountain point in the French Alps is Mont Blanc.

276. Tulips are a member of the lily family of flowers.

277. The song "Killing an Arab" by the alternative rock band The Cure was inspired by Albert Camus' novel *The Stranger*.

278. Men are statistically more likely to die from cancer than women.

279. Kleenex brand tissues were invented in 1924, but facial tissues were first used by the Japanese predating the 17th century.

280. Pop star Miley Cyrus was born Destiny Hope Cyrus.

281. Chlorine bleach is most effective as a disinfectant when diluting with water and then allowing the target to air dry.

282. The Dust Bowl describes both the region of the United States and the time period in which it affected its inhabitants during the 1930s.

283. There are 23 distinct provinces in the People's Republic of China.

284. One cup of raw kale contains more Vitamin C than one orange.

285. Adirondack chairs are known as muskoka chairs in regions of Canada.

286. Loon Mountain Ski Resort in Lincoln, New Hampshire, has 370 skiable acres of property.

287. Ovaltine, the malted milk flavoring powder, was invented in Switzerland.

288. Baasha is a traditional South Asian candy.

289. The world record time for climbing Mount Everest is eight hours and ten minutes.

290. Tightrope walking, a circus discipline based on balance, is also known as funambulism.

291. R.L. Stine, born Robert Lawrence Stine, has used other pen names during his career. These include Jovial Bob Stine and Eric Affabee.

292. Sir Patrick Stewart, famous for his role as Captain Jean-Luc Picard in the television series *Star Trek,* was a member of the Royal Shakespeare Company from 1966 to 1982.

293. National Chocolate Chip Day is on May 14th, but National Chocolate Chip Cookie Day is on August 4th.

294. Jacob and WIlhelm Grimm, better known as the Brothers Grimm, were the first to publish famous stories such as *Cinderella* and *Rapunzel,* but they were primarily linguists.

295. The jerboa, a desert rodent found commonly in the Sahara Desert and other comparable climates, both looks and moves like a kangaroo apart from its size.

296. The largest recorded ostrich egg weighed just under 5 pounds and 12 ounces. It was produced by an ostrich in Sweden.

297. The top three producers of wine in the world, in order, are France, Italy, and the United States.

298. A triphthong is a vowel sound that combines three different vowel sounds into a single utterance.

299. In medieval times, a chandler was someone who was in charge of making, storing, and accounting for wax and candles in the household. The chandelier is named after this role.

300. VH1's *Top 20 Video Countdown* was the longest running music program of its kind, airing from 1994 through 2015.

301. The Blackjack Hall of Fame can be found at the Barona Resort and Casino in San Diego, California.

302. The three countries in the world which have not adopted the metric system as their primary

measurement system are the United States, Myanmar (Burma), and Liberia.

303. There are 25 species of hamsters.

304. Porcelain is a subset of ceramic and was first mastered by the Chinese during the 1300s.

305. The brand Muzak specializes in the genre of elevator and background music.

306. One of the first famous freak show attractions of Europe were Johannes and Lazarus Baptista Colloredo, who were conjoined twins joined at the chest.

307. Approximately 65% of the world drives on the right-hand side of the road, while the other 35% drive on the left-hand side.

308. Homing pigeons are trained to carry up to 75 grams on their backs during flight.

309. The original names for the common sports bra were first jockbra and jogbra.

310. The name for flip flops, the popular open-toe sandal, is an example of onomatopoeia, in that they were named after the sound they make as they hit your foot while you walk.

311. Candy apples were invented in 1908. Their cousin, the caramel apple, was invented in 1950's.

312. The Marlboro Man mascot of Marlboro cigarettes was a marketing strategy designed to give their products a masculine appeal. Before his reveal, Marlboro was seen as a women's brand.

313. Robert Goddard, who invented the liquid fueled rocket, was inspired by the science fiction novel *The War of The Worlds*.

314. The *Curious George* children's book series was created by two people. Margaret Reyes is the credited author while her husband, Hans Agusto (H.A.) Reyes, is credited with illustration.

315. The most direct path to swim across the English Channel from England to France measures 21 miles.

316. Moxibustion is the process of burning mugwort on parts of the body, either directly or via acupuncture needles, as a form of healing. Along with acupuncture, it is one of

the oldest forms of traditional Chinese medicine still in practice.

317. The Red Hat Society is an American women's organization, initially targeted at women ages 50 and older, that seeks to create and foster female social networks.

318. Radio and television personality Glenn Beck received his first on-air gig at the age of 13.

319. The Random House Publishing Company received its name because the original founders only planned on releasing a handful of works in their spare time. It is now the largest publisher of general-interest literature in the world.

320. Multi-level marketing strategies and pyramid schemes are almost identical in structure, but the former has a specific focus on buying and selling physical product.

321. The Louie Awards, more formally known as the International Greeting Cards Award Competition, annually seeks to recognize the year's best greeting cards.

322. Ice must be at least four inches thick to bear human weight.

323. Romani gypsies' first ancestors came from India.

324. The system of measuring mass that utilizes pounds and ounces is technically referred to as the avoirdupois system.

325. In the hit television series *Breaking Bad*, protagonist Walter White's alter ego name, Heisenberg, is a tribute to physicist Werner Heisenberg.

326. Liquid and dry measuring cups take up the same amount of volume.

327. Approximately two percent of the world's population has naturally blond hair.

328. Tennis star Maria Sharapova founded and owns her own candy company called Sugarpova.

329. Jim Harrigan was an American juggling artist who specialized in manipulating cigar boxes.

330. There are different shapes for wine glasses depending on whether you are drinking a red

wine or a white wine. For red wine, the glass is typically larger.

331. Approximately 10% of the world's population identifies as left-handed.

332. The Native American Hoop Dance competition occurs every year in Phoenix, Arizona, at the Heard Museum.

333. When dragonflies mate, they create a shape called "the mating wheel," that resembles a heart.

334. When John Waters' film *Pink Flamingos* was first released, it was banned in Australia, Norway, and parts of Canada due to its radical content.

335. The first woman to graduate from Vanderbilt University Law School was Pauline LaFon Gore, mother to politician Al Gore.

336. The official national sport of the Kingdom of Bhutan is archery.

337. There is an annual marathon across the North Pole known as the North Pole Marathon. The first event was in 2002.

338. The middle initial in Ulysses S. Grant's name did not stand for anything; it was the result of a records accident which was never resolved.

339. Families of fallen service members were not allowed to put the encircled pentagram symbol on the tombstones of their loved ones until 2007.

340. Judy Garland was paid $500 for her role in *The Wizard of Oz*.

341. French fries were first brought to the United States by President Thomas Jefferson in 1801.

342. The lids of mason jars are only meant to be used once when canning. However, the band and jar are both reusable.

343. The largest recorded earthquake in the world occurred in Chile in 1960. It was a 9.5 magnitude earthquake.

344. Jim Crow laws were named after a satirical blackface song and dance called "Jump Jim Crow," which was performed in 1832.

345. Harvey Milk served in the United States Navy before he became a politician.

346. After the 2003 Great Northeast Blackout, communities in Ontario participated in a Voluntary Blackout Day Challenge to commemorate the event. It was an annual event until 2010.

347. Grandmaster Flash and the Furious Five opened for The Clash at two concerts in May of 1981.

348. The educational television series *Schoolhouse Rock* was first named *Scholastic Rock*, until the publishing company Scholastic Inc. acquired the rights to the title and forced the change to occur.

349. The address 123 Sesame Street is set in the Upper West Side of Manhattan, New York.

350. The Goths and Visigoths strategically destroyed the ancient Roman aqueducts during their invasions.

351. The town in *Family Guy* is designed to resemble the scenery in Cranston, Rhode Island.

352. Rapper Jay-Z attended the same high school as Notorious B.I.G. and Busta Rhymes in Brooklyn, New York.

353. Justin Trudeau taught high school French, drama, and math before becoming a politician.

354. In 2009, a web series called *The Andrew Show* aired, with the mission of spreading white supremacy values to children. It was hosted by Andrew Pendergraft, grandson to Thom Robb, who is the director of the Knights of the Ku Klux Klan.

355. There are two different dates for National Pie Day; December 1st and January 23rd. National Pi Day, however, is March 14th.

356. Early cartographers would include fake towns on their maps in order to catch forgers illegally duplicating their work.

357. Handbag is both a noun and a verb.

358. Former president Richard Nixon could play piano, saxophone, violin, clarinet, and accordion.

359. One of Joseph Gordon Levitt's first filmed appearances was in a television advertisement for Cocoa Puffs cereal.

360. The Hebrew calendar is organized so that Jewish New Year never occurs on a Sunday.

361. The first version of the QWERTY keyboard was created in the early 1870s.

362. The first product ever sold by Motorola was a battery eliminator.

363. Walkie talkies were developed for use in World War II.

364. The Muzzy language learning series, created by the BBC, has been translated into six different languages, including Mandarin.

365. Johnny Bravo, the protagonist of the Cartoon Network series *Johnny Bravo*, was named after a Brady Bunch episode.

366. Over-ingesting zinc can result in decreased absorption of copper and iron by the body.

367. Both men and women can contract toxic shock syndrome, even though it is typically associated with only women.

368. Gargoyles were first invented as water spouts to carry rainwater away from the edges of stone buildings to protect the masonry. Purely decorative gargoyles are called chimeras.

369. The first taxidermy competition in the United States was in 1880. The winning piece was two Bornean orangutans fighting over a female figure.

370. The only place in the world one can review slides of Albert Einstein's brain is at the Mütter Museum in Philadelphia, Pennsylvania.

371. The Mall of America is home to 520 individual stores.

372. North Korea has 28 pre-approved haircuts for its citizens.

373. In feng shui, it is unlucky to place your bed directly opposite to your door because it mimics the position in which the dead are carried through open doors.

374. Wicca is a subset of Paganism invented in England in the middle of the 20th century.

375. One serving of spaghetti squash has 20 calories.

376. Coulrophobia is the fear of clowns.

377. The Ukulele Orchestra of Great Britain consists of 9 musicians.

378. Pug dogs sleep for an average of 14 hours every day.

379. The restaurant located in the disk of the Seattle Space Needle rotates. It can complete a full 360-degree rotation in under an hour.

380. When it was built, the Trump International Hotel and Tower was the 7th tallest building in the world.

381. June Jordan's novel *His Own Where* was the first full-novel to use only African American Vernacular English, more commonly referred to as Ebonics.

382. Baby pandas do not open their eyes until approximately six to eight weeks after birth.

383. Himalayan pink salt receives its color from the presence of iron oxide.

384. Goats have rectangular pupils which give them a range of vision from 320 to 340 degrees.

385. Packing peanuts are colored based on their makeup. Green peanuts contain at least 70% recycled polystyrene, white peanuts contain at least 70% un-recycled polystyrene, and pink peanuts are anti-static.

386. Arizona allows citizens to openly carry guns, yet it is illegal to carry nunchucks.

387. The metal band which connects the pencil to the eraser on its end is called a ferrule.

388. One of the first iterations of the computer mouse had the cord extending from the back of the device, inspiring its name.

389. Skeleton keys received their name not because they resemble the bumps and ridges of spinal vertebrae, but because they have been reduced to their core essential elements.

390. The opening sequence for *The Matrix* took four days to shoot.

391. Keanu Reeves was born in Beirut, Lebanon.

392. There is a website dedicated to grafting the image of Steve Buscemi's eyes on famous celebrities called "Chicks with Steve Buscemeyes."

393. The Hershey's chocolate factory makes 70 million Hershey Kisses every day.

394. Heinz sells approximately 11 billion single-serving ketchup packets every year, enough for every person living on Earth to have two.

395. Conjoined twins are born in roughly 1 in 50,000 human pregnancies.

396. In Australian slang, a charley horse is called a corky.

397. Don Ed Hardy, famous for his clothing line brand and collaborations, studied classical Japanese tattoo techniques in the 1970s.

398. The Food and Drug Administration (FDA) requires any product labeled as a multivitamin to contain at least 3 vitamins or minerals.

399. The town of Nagoro, Japan, is inhabited by more scarecrows than humans.

400. Approximately 70% of the kangaroo meat farmed in Australia is exported overseas, particularly to Europe.

401. Hispanic and Latino are the only ethnic categories currently available on the US Census survey.

402. The Japanese Prime Minister, Shinzo Abe, studied politics at the University of Southern California from 1977 to 1979.

403. *Napoleon Dynamite* was filmed in both Idaho and Utah. The entire film took 22 days to shoot.

404. It is illegal to fish for, sell, or trade any and all shark products in the Bahamas.

405. Roderick Jaynes, the editor credited in several films by the Coen brothers including *Fargo, No Country for Old Men, The Ladykillers, O Brother, Where Art Thou?* and more, does not exist. He is a pen name for the brothers themselves.

406. The phrase "o'clock" is derived from "stroke of the clock." The latter refers to mechanical clocks used during the Medieval period.

407. China, Laos, Vietnam, and Cuba, although governed by Communist leaders, all technically identify as Socialist nations.

408. It is illegal to whistle, yell, or sing loudly on public streets in Sullivan's Island, South Carolina, especially between the times of 11PM

and 7AM. It is considered a disturbance of the peace.

409. The all-black uniform of a ninja is called a shinobi shozoku.

410. Snake skin contains keratin, the protein found in human hair. It gives snakeskin its trademark shine.

411. Ringo Starr, the best-known drummer of The Beatles, was born Richard Starkey. The first drummer for the Beatles was Pete Best.

412. Cerebral palsy affects 1 in 323 children in the United States.

413. The postal code 12345 belongs to General Electric, specifically located in Schenectady, New York.

414. The first door locks were invented by the ancient Egyptians.

415. Aluminum can be recycled and put back on store shelves in about 60 days, glass in 30 days.

416. Both the stickers and glue found on produce are made from edible-grade, FDA approved materials.

417. Both male and female reindeer, called Caribou in North America, grow antlers.

418. Adult lice are approximately the size of a sesame seed and lay 3 to 4 eggs per day.

419. Like gymnasts, bull riders commonly use rosin to improve their grip.

420. The first manufactured cereal was called granula. It was the predecessor to modern day granola.

421. The late Steve Jobs was adopted at an early age.

422. German Chancellor Angela Merkel studied physics and quantum chemistry before becoming a politician.

423. Volcanic eruptions and lightning strikes create the compounds which, together, result in acid rain.

424. Former speaker of the house John Boehner grew up with 11 siblings and was the first in his family to attend college.

425. The Comfort Tree is the oldest sugar maple tree in Canada at approximately 500 years of age.

426. Pine cones contain the reproductive structures of their bearers and are classified as either male or female.

427. Drinking chocolate dates back to Mayan culture in the mid-400s AD.

428. At Lake Superior State University, you can apply for and receive an official unicorn hunting license.

429. The castle of *Downton Abbey* is named Highclere Castle and has belonged to the Cavernon family since 1679.

430. Dothraki, the language in *Game of Thrones*, is a real, learnable language thanks to linguist David J. Peterson.

431. New Zealand is home to the world's largest insect, the giant weta.

432. Sports brand Nike was named after the goddess Nike, who symbolized victory.

433. The official LiveJournal mascot is Frank the Goat.

434. Outside of his rock band Fall Out Boy, Pete Wentz has led several large projects including a

clothing line and a bar, and he has authored several books.

435. Both the iconic yellow color and low-tack glue of post-it notes were made by mistake. The glue was meant to be an extra-strong formula for another project, while the paper color was initially from available scrap paper.

436. Joe Biden ran for president of the United States in both 1987 and 2008.

437. Cereal giant Quaker Oats is based in Cedar Rapids, Iowa.

438. In the United Kingdom, stamps bear the profile image of the monarch but not the name of the country. It is the only country to not put its name on its stamps.

439. The first flushing toilet was invented in 1596. The inventor, John Harrington, inspired its casual label, the john.

440. There is a museum in Peaks Island, Maine, dedicated exclusively to umbrella covers. It is home to over 700 pieces.

441. In *The Simpsons*, God and Jesus are the only characters throughout the series who are drawn with five fingers on each hand.

442. *Flight of the Conchords* first aired as a radio program through the BBC before it was picked up by HBO for television.

443. The North Star is officially known as Polaris. It is also the last point of the 'handle' of the Little Dipper constellation.

444. Vega is predicted to become the new North Star in approximately 12,000 years.

445. Herman Cain simultaneously worked for the US Navy developing ballistics while also completing his Master in Science for Computer Studies at Purdue University.

446. The first language of the Governor of Maine, Paul LePage, was French.

447. In 2016, over one-third of Americans report that they have listened to a podcast. In 2006, only one-tenth reported doing so.

448. Roald Dahl was significantly involved in World War II. He was first a fighter pilot for the Royal Air Force, then a British diplomat,

and later a spy for MI6. He left the service in 1946.

449. England experimented with anarchism following the collapse of the established government after the English Civil War.

450. The Confederate flag was designed and first flown in Alabama.

451. There is virtually no record of William Shakespeare in historical documents from 1585 to 1592.

452. Anderson Cooper was a model under Ford Models from age 10 to age 13.

453. Another name for the avocado is the alligator pear, due to its skin texture and shape.

454. The protein pikachurin was named after the character Pikachu.

455. The plot for the film *O Brother, Where Art Thou?* by the Coen brothers is derived from Homer's *Odyssey*.

456. CNN was the first cable television station devoted specifically to news programming in the United States and the first in the world to offer 24-hour news coverage.

457. The United States two-dollar bill was not printed from 1966 to 1976.

458. Afghans are named after their first documented creators, the people of Afghanistan.

459. The Pantone Color of the Year in 2002 was True Red.

460. Leo Fender, founder of Fender Electric Instrument Manufacturing Company, was a saxophonist and never learned how to play the guitars his business crafted.

461. The term spirits, in reference to distilled alcoholic beverages, was inspired by Middle Eastern alchemy. When alchemists conducted experiments, the vapors produced during the process were called the spirit of the original product.

462. Under the official Wimbledon dress code, all athletes are required to wear all white, with no variant colors, no panels of non-white color, and no company or brand logos.

463. In synchronized swimming, performers are not allowed to touch the bottom of the pool during the routine.

464. The first revolving door was installed in Times Square in 1899.

465. Nikola Tesla, who discovered AC electric power, was born during a lightning storm.

466. David Beckham left school to play for the junior team of Manchester United when he was just 16 years old.

467. In 1971, Larry King was arrested on charges of grand larceny.

468. Swiss law prohibits its bankers from disclosing confidential information without the account holder's consent.

469. The Chinese Gold Panda is a gold bullion coin produced by the mint of China. The obverse design remains the same, but the reverse sees a new panda design every year.

470. In the wild, sloths grow algae on their fur, which acts to camouflage them.

471. The US Army guidelines state that enlistees must have all 10 toes to be considered for service.

472. The original Chelsea boot dates to 1851 and was invented and patented by Queen Victoria's shoemaker, J. Sparkes-Hall.

473. Humans lose an average of 50 to 100 strands of hair daily.

474. Brad Pitt was born in Oklahoma but grew up in Missouri.

475. There are twenty-one performers who have been inducted into the Rock and Roll Hall of Fame more than once.

476. The standardization of women's clothing size measurements became privatized in 1995 by ASTM International.

477. Bangladesh is home to over 1,000 citizens per square kilometer.

478. Actress Julie Andrews' big movie break was as the titular character in Disney's adaptation of *Mary Poppins*.

479. The television series *Twin Peaks* was set in Washington State, but was initially planned to bet set in North Dakota.

480. In 1973, actor Marlon Brando declined his Academy Award for Best Actor for his performance in *The Godfather*. Instead, a Native American civil rights activist named Sacheen Littlefeather gave a speech on his behalf criticizing the Academy for its historically negative depiction and treatment of Native Americans.

481. Cases of Lyme disease have been found and reported on every continent except for Antarctica.

482. Pakistan and Afghanistan are the last two nations in the world still struggling with wild polio cases.

483. The last public execution by guillotine occurred in 1939. The last private one, however, was in 1977.

484. The Krusty Krab in the children's television series *SpongeBob SquarePants* is modeled after a real-life crab cage used in fishing.

485. The state with the most churches per capita is North Dakota.

486. Dogs and some cats can 'catch' the yawns of their owners.

487. In basketball, the POSS statistic is short for 'possible', not 'pause'.

488. Ice hockey transitioned from being played in 2 halves to 3 periods in 1910.

489. Web content is information-based, while web copy is persuasion-based.

490. Peter Dinklage is 4' 5" tall.

491. Surrealism was primarily a literary movement before it became an art movement.

492. One of the victims of the mysterious Dyatlov Pass Incident, Lyudmila Alexandrovna Dubinina, was found dead and missing her tongue, eyes, parts of her lips, some facial tissue, and a portion of her skull bone.

493. The Man in the Iron Mask, a famous French prisoner during the mid-17th century, was held under the same jailer for 34 years.

494. The metal band Iron Maiden is named after a popular Medieval torture device. The device

was an iron coffin outfitted with spikes designed to pierce the victim.

495. In 1912, Japan donated over 3,000 cherry trees to the United States as a symbol of friendship. Those trees were planted in Washington, D.C.

496. The character Big Daddy in Tennessee Williams' play *Cat on a Hot Tin Roof* was based on his own father.

497. Nashville, Tennessee, was founded on the Christmas Eve of 1779.

498. The human hamstring 'muscle' is a composite of three separate muscles in the posterior of the leg: semitendinosus, semimembranosus, and the bicep femoris.

499. Jackie Chan is mostly known for starring in several successful martial arts movies but also has had a successful music career. He trained at the Peking Opera School as a child and has released 20 studio albums.

500. The long barrack portion of the Alamo was the first recorded hospital in Spanish Texas. It is now a museum.

501. Colorado state legislation dictates that any points accumulated due to driving misconduct will stay on the driver's record for seven years.

502. Micronesia is a region of Oceania consisting of thousands of small islands. The Federated States of Micronesia are an even smaller sub region and contains only the states of Yap, Chuuk, Pohnpei, and Kosrae.

503. S.O.S., the Morse code signal for help, is not an acronym of any larger morphemes.

504. The middle finger as a vulgar gesture dates back to Ancient Rome as a phallic and aggressive gesture.

505. In 1970, jewelry company Cartier projected a holographic image of a hand covered in jewels onto the sidewalk outside their New York City location as an advertisement.

506. Mary, Queen of Scots, used invisible ink during her 18-year house arrest to correspond with her supporters.

507. The first appointed Chief of Surgery of Johns Hopkins Hospital invented rubber gloves. His name was William Stewart Halsted.

508. The Cambodian flag features an image of Angkor Wat, the largest temple in Angkor.

509. The MTV Video Music Awards (VMA's) were first awarded in 1984.

510. Comedian and actor Jack Black is the son of two satellite engineers.

511. In mythology, mermaids are half-human and half-fish. Sirens, however, are half-human and half-bird.

512. Monaco claims the greatest life expectancy rate, at 89.52 years. Chad has the lowest, at 49.81 years.

513. The Black Hand was a Serbian secret military that was tied to the assassination of Archduke Franz Ferdinand in Sarajevo. Subsequently, they are considered to be one of the contributing factors to the cause of the Great War.

514. Tea is the second most commonly consumed beverage in the world. Water is the most consumed beverage.

515. There are an estimated 300 or more different languages of sign language throughout the world.

516. Keloid scars, which are built-up masses of collagen, are 15 times more likely to affect persons of African descent in comparison to those of European descent. Keloids were first described by Ancient Egyptian surgeons around 1700 B.C.E.

517. Contact lenses were first conceptualized by artist Leonardo da Vinci but would not be created until 1887. The first contact lenses were made with glass.

518. The signature dish of the casual restaurant chain Applebee's is their riblets.

519. The United States used to have two separate and competing official jump rope organizations, but in 1995 they merged and became the United States Amateur Jump Rope Federation.

520. Spandex, both the brand and the term, are an anagram of the word 'expands'.

521. Clint Eastwood is the descendant of a Mayflower passenger named William Bradford.

522. Former presidents Theodore "Teddy" Roosevelt and Franklin Delano Roosevelt were fifth cousins.

523. Theodore Roosevelt founded the Progressive Party, later nicknamed the Bull Moose Party, in 1912.

524. The company John Deere, now famous for its tractors and plows, also made covered wagons during the 19th century when they were commonly used by pioneers traveling west.

525. Mormon doctrine forbids the consumption of alcohol, coffee, tea, or any other caffeinated beverages.

526. The original rhinestones were found in the river Rhine and were made of rock crystal.

527. The four modern precious gemstones are emerald, ruby, sapphire, and diamond. All other gemstones are classified as semi-precious.

528. The average modern electronic device contains over 35 different minerals.

529. Wind turbine towers measure approximately 260 feet tall on average. For comparison, Sacré Coeur Basilica in Paris, France, measures 273 feet tall at its highest point.

530. Jane Fonda has been married and divorced three times.

531. Egypt is the only nation within the Middle East located on the African continent.

532. Former US Secretary of State Condoleezza Rice enrolled as a student University of Denver when she was 15 years old.

533. Morgan Freeman is a beekeeper in his free time. He owns and maintains 26 hives.

534. The earliest forms of food for astronauts came in toothpaste-like tubes. Modern space food now highly resembles typical civilian fare.

535. The Salvation Army was founded by English Methodists William and Catherine Booth. They now are present in 127 countries around the world.

536. The late actor Chris Farley was the original top pick to voice the titular ogre in *Shrek*.

537. The total distance of the Union Pacific Railroad Company's routes is 32,100 miles.

538. The legal age for horse and dog race betting in the state of Kentucky is 18.

539. The popular lottery game keno was first introduced to casinos in the 1930s but was first conceived of by the ancient Chinese.

540. Australia has the highest gambling rate in the world, at 80% of the population citing they engage in some form of gambling. Winnings throughout Australia are not taxed.

541. Begonia plants fall under the same order, *Cucurbitales*, as melons, squash, and pumpkins.

542. Jelly Roll Morton, one of the early pioneers of jazz music, was a racial mix of African, French, and Spanish descent.

543. The largest rubber duck ever made measures 54 feet tall and lives in Buffalo, New York.

544. Before the invention of modern glitter, mica, hematite, powdered galema, and beetles were used to achieve a similar effect.

545. The two lifts judged in Olympic level weightlifting are the clean-and-jerk and the snatch.

546. In ancient Greece, one game involved running while wearing partial armor. It was a men's game.

547. Former president William Taft is credited for starting the ceremonial first pitch tradition in baseball. Since then, every serving president has thrown at least one of these pitches.

548. Napoleon Bonaparte attempted, and failed, at committing suicide after being sentenced to exile in Elba.

549. There are eight different types of nipples.

550. Scotland has the highest prevalence rate of cocaine in the world in its population. It is estimated that 1 in 40 Scots use cocaine.

551. The film genre of spaghetti westerns is referred to as macaroni westerns in Japan. Some Italians refer to them as westerns *all'italiana*.

552. The television series *M.A.S.H.* holds the record for the most watched series finale. It drew an audience of over 121 million viewers.

553. In 1999 the NSA banned Furbies from their campus out of concern they could be used to record and consequently transmit confidential information.

554. While filming the original *Willy Wonka and the Chocolate Factory*, director Mel Stuart often would not reveal the set or tone of a scene to the cast in order to get their genuine reactions on film.

555. All the volcanic eruptions which have occurred in the contiguous United States over the last 200 years have come from volcanoes in the Cascade Mountain Range.

556. The median age of West Virginia residents is 41.

557. Styrofoam is a brand, not a material. The material, which makes insulated single-use coffee and food containers, is technically polystyrene foam.

558. The first 'L' in salmonella is pronounced.

559. Humans are most likely to contract Mad Cow Disease if they eat the brain or spinal cord tissue of an infected animal. It is much less likely when eating muscle or dairy product.

560. A cluster of cats is called a clowder.

561. Female widow spiders are known for eating the male after mating, inspiring the 'widow' name. This behavior is technically known as sexual cannibalism.

562. The first patented garbage disposal was called the InSinkErator.

563. Throughout the world, a death by suicide occurs approximately every 40 seconds.

564. In Lancaster, Pennsylvania, the local Costco has a designated horse and buggy parking area for its Amish customers.

565. The red-light district in New Orleans in the beginning of the 20th century was known as Storyville, named after the councilman organized it, Alderman Sidney Story.

566. The three 'Progressive Presidents' who oversaw the public move towards social and political reform in the early 20th century were

Theodore Roosevelt, William Taft, and Woodrow Wilson.

567. Titanium (III) chloride is a compound which appears as a royal purple liquid.

568. The iconic yellow color of the North American school bus was instituted in 1939.

569. Paris Hilton's highest completed level of education is a GED.

570. Former football player O.J. Simpson is Kim Kardashian's godfather.

571. Sixteen people have gone over the edge of Niagara Falls intentionally since the first attempt in 1901, and eleven of those people have survived the fall. It is illegal to attempt this feat and carries a fine of $10,000.

572. Women make up approximately 24% of the STEM field jobs in the United States.

573. Ice skating as an activity and a sport was pioneered by the British, but modern figure skating was developed by an American named Jackson Haines.

574. John Krasinski was an intern for *Late Night with Conan O'Brien* at NBC before getting his big break as Jim Halpert in *The Office*.

575. The bestselling beer in the world is Snow Beer, a lager made and distributed almost exclusively in China.

576. Under the Civil Liberties Act, all Japanese Americans and respective heirs who survived the internment camps during World War II were issued $20,000 as an apology on behalf of the U.S. government.

577. There were 23 recorded suicide attempts by inmates at the Guantanamo Bay detention camp in August of 2003.

578. New Zealand was the first nation to allow women to vote. The Grand Duchy of Finland, which is now the Republic of Finland, was the first to allow women to both vote and run for parliament.

579. Ocean Avenue is both the subject matter of rock band Yellowcard's breakout single and also the setting of *The Amityville Horror*.

580. Caterpillars, like snakes, commonly shed their skin as they grow.

581. One in every 23 million people are legitimately allergic to water.

582. The Koch snowflake is one of the earliest articulations of a fractal. Its first iteration resembles the Star of David.

583. The word 'barbecue' functions as both a noun, verb, and adjective.

584. The letters 'l' and 'r' are phonological minimal pairs. They are both alveolar consonants, but 'l' is a lateral consonant while 'r' is a retroflex consonant.

585. The most common beer bottle color is dark brown because it keeps the contents fresher for longer by deflecting UV light.

586. Whole wheat flour is generally more absorbent than white flour.

587. The first film adaption of Mary Shelley's *Frankenstein* was a 15-minute silent film by Thomas Edison.

588. The paisley print is named after the town of Paisley in West Scotland, although its roots are Persian.

589. The African country of Liberia was founded when the United States began to resettle freed southern slaves on the African coast in the early 1800s before the beginning of the American Civil War. Liberia is Latin for "Land of the Free".

590. 'Bureau' and 'dresser' refer to the same piece of furniture.

591. The Eiffel Tower was constructed as a monument to the centennial of the French Revolution. It was first opened to the public during the French World Fair in 1889.

592. Maria Montessori was the first female doctor in Italy. She graduated from the University of Rome in 1896, and her dissertation was published in 1897.

593. An all-white peacock is typically leucistic, a condition which results in a loss of pigmentation but is not the same as albinism.

594. Gelato has less cream and less fat than ice cream, but more sugar.

595. Benito Mussolini was named after Benito Juárez, the left-wing Mexican president of the mid-1800s.

596. The Netherlands was the first country to legalize same-sex marriage.

597. Autism is approximately four or five more times likely to affect boys than girls.

598. King Henry IV was the youngest person to ever ascend the English throne at 9 months old.

599. Daniel Ford Burnham is most well-known for planning and executing the World's Columbian Exposition in 1893, but was also a leading architect for many other famous structures in the United States and the Philippines.

600. The citizens of Falkland Islands celebrate Margaret Thatcher Day every year to celebrate her saving the colony from an Argentinian takeover in 1983.

601. The influenza pandemic of 1918 was a global phenomenon which affected approximately

500 million people throughout the world and was rated the highest possible value on the Pandemic Severity Index.

602. Female Tasmanian Devils can bear up to 50 pups at once, but only four can survive, one for each available teat in her pouch.

603. Tasmania was home to the first official Green Party, named the United Tasmania Group.

604. The late author John Steinbeck served as a news correspondent for the *New York Herald Tribune* during World War II.

605. The late Upton Sinclair used his earnings from his successful novel *The Jungle* to build and found a socialist community called the Helicone Home Colony, which was destroyed by a fire one year later.

606. It is a tradition throughout Peru to give friends and family yellow underpants on New Year's Eve.

607. The original rubber ducks were designed to be chew toys, not bath toys.

608. PEZ candies were initially just mints designed to help smokers kick their unhealthy habits.

Their name comes from the German *pfefferminz,* or peppermint.

609. The first recorded reference to a thong in the United States was in 1939. The mayor of New York, Fiorello LaGuardia, required nude dancers to wear them for decency.

610. Airplane pilots have nicknamed LaGuardia Airport in New York, New York, the USS LaGuardia because its short runways and watery surrounds are reminiscent of landing on an aircraft carrier at sea.

611. America's Independence Day was first declared on July 2, 1776, but it took two days for Congress to accept Thomas Jefferson's declaration, resulting in the now commonly celebrated 4th of July.

612. The first barcode patents ever issued described both linear and bullseye shaped patterns.

613. *The Picture of Dorian Gray* was Oscar Wilde's only novel.

614. Although both coffins and caskets are designed for housing dead bodies, coffins have

two more sides than a casket. Also, caskets are typically designed with a split lid, making viewing the deceased easier at the wake.

615. Hamper is another term for basket and is traditionally made of wicker.

616. The first self-service laundry station was called a washateria, a term still used in Texas.

617. Pope Francis is both the first Jesuit pope and the first from the Americas to lead the papacy.

618. Melania Trump, current wife of Donald Trump, can speak five languages: English, French, German, Serbian, and Slovenian, which is her native language.

619. Fairy cakes are a British variant of American cupcakes. They are generally slightly smaller and less ornately decorated.

620. Although the Black Plague peaked in Europe in the middle of the 14th century, evidence suggests it originated in Central Asia.

621. Many commercial brand toothpastes contain sodium lauryl sulfate, the same foaming agent found in many shampoos.

622. According to the FDA, plain deodorant is classified as a cosmetic, but antiperspirant deodorant is an over-the-counter drug.

623. In order to apply as an astronaut at NASA, you must have at least 1,000 hours of logged flying time as a pilot in-command in a jet aircraft, as well as a minimum of a bachelor's degree in biology, engineering, physical science, or mathematics.

624. The Soviet space program was split between Russia and Ukraine after the fall of the Soviet Union, resulting in two separate organizations.

625. The Great Leap Forward was Mao Zedong's first move in what became the Cultural Revolution. Its spectacular failure to produce the goods and culture desired resulted in the Great Chinese Famine.

626. During the initial pressing and releasing of Reggie and the Full Effect's 2003 album *Under the Tray*, the CD was hidden under the tray rather than in its customary resting place.

627. Straight edge culture and values were most publicly advocated by the American hardcore punk band Minor Threat in the 1980s.

628. Plastic bags do not begin to degrade until approximately 700 years have passed.

629. The use of Christmas trees is rooted in Protestant Christian traditions.

630. The character of Norman Bates was inspired by the story of murderer and body snatcher Ed Gein.

631. During the early 1900s, the vice industry of the Sunset Strip thrived because it fell under the jurisdiction of the local sheriff's department rather than the powerful LAPD.

632. Michigan was the first state in the United States to actively fluoridate its public drinking water.

633. Snakes are able to hear via sound wave vibrations that their bodies pick up.

634. Melvil Dewey was both the inventor of the Dewey Decimal Classification System as well as a founding member of the American Library Association.

635. African slavery thrived in Latin America before it became common in North America.

636. The cardboard sleeve required to cook Hot Pockets in a microwave oven is called a susceptor.

637. The original chalkboards were made with slate, but modern ones are typically made with porcelain enameled steel.

638. The ancestor of the chalkboard was the personal writing slate, dating as far back as the 11th century. In comparison, whiteboards were not invented until the 1950s.

639. It is an urban myth that drinking seltzer water leaches calcium from your bones.

640. One serving of eggnog contains over 200 calories.

641. The first motorized police car was large enough to fit an entire town's police force, inspiring the term 'squad car.' It was built in 1899 and destroyed one year later.

642. Before being used as the name of a water vessel, the word 'submarine' was used as an

adjective to describe something as being underwater.

643. Martha Graham danced for 50 years and had a career which lasted 75 years.

644. Jim Gaffigan is known as a 'clean' comedian in that his material contains minimal profanity.

645. There is no known historically direct relation between the country names of Australia and Austria.

646. The name for the original Walkman was inspired by the comic book hero Superman.

647. The highest possible score in the Pac-Man video game is 3,333,360 points.

648. The characters in the *Teletubbies* BBC children's series were designed after astronauts in their space suits. Each character had slightly different yet distinct facial skin color for intentional diversity.

649. The largest recorded number of completed cat's cradle changes is 22,700.

650. The Cirque du Soleil first appeared in Las Vegas in 1992 with their show *Nouvelle Expérience*. They now have six active permanent

residency shows throughout Las Vegas and three shows retired from that area.

651. The famous gangster John Dillinger entered the US Navy in the early 1920s to avoid being arrested for his first offense but left the service after less than a year.

652. Jack the Ripper is one of the most well-known and iconic serial killers in modern history, but his true identity is still unknown.

653. The longest running Broadway show in history is *Phantom of the Opera*. Runners up, in order, are *Chicago, The Lion King, Cats,* and *Les Misérables*.

654. Novelist Jane Austen's first collection of works is called *Juvenilia* and contains works from her youth.

655. The Disney World Epcot theme park in Florida was designed to model a future utopian society. Epcot is an acronym for 'Experimental Prototype Community of Tomorrow."

656. Pop singer Cyndi Lauper was the artist behind the theme song for the children's television series *Pee Wee's Playhouse*.

657. The five cases of Latin grammar are nominative, genitive, dative, accusative, and ablative.

658. The Pasadena Chalk Festival is the largest annual sidewalk chalk festival in the world. Its first event was in 1993.

659. Redwood trees have existed on Earth for approximately 240 million years, predating flowers and birds.

660. In Japan, one can buy a life-sized replica of oneself in gummy candy form from the FabCafe for approximately $65 USD.

661. The lyrics of "Circle of Life," the opening track for *The Lion King,* are written and sung in Zulu.

662. The dessert spoon as a unit of culinary measure is abbreviated to 'dstspn' and equates to approximately 2 teaspoons.

663. Thomas Jefferson, the third president of the United States, is recognized as the inventor of the swivel chair.

664. During the prohibition of capoeira practice in Brazil at the end of the 19th century,

capoeiristas would quickly switch from capoeira to samba dance when police were on the way to avoid punishment.

665. Belly dance is both a performance art and a form of social dance in the Middle East.

666. Velvet worms have tiny claws on each foot which can be retracted when walking on smooth surfaces. Their 'velvet' texture is made of bristles which provide information about sound and smell.

667. The earliest ancestors of confetti as an item thrown in celebration are fruit, nuts, coins, and mud balls. Mud and eggs were usually thrown by lower-class citizens as a way of mocking the upper-class nobles.

668. Although former US President Dwight D. Eisenhower was a highly regarded five-star general in the US Army who served in both World Wars, he never saw active combat.

669. The Soviet Union owned the rights to the classic video game Tetris until 1996.

670. Bob Ross primarily used the 'wet on wet' oil painting technique, as notable artists Monet,

Rembrandt, and Fragonard also used in their own works.

671. MLB superstar Barry Bonds' godfather is another famous MLB player, Willie Mays.

672. Another name for the element mercury is quicksilver, because of its appearance in liquid form.

673. Albert Einstein postulated the existence of black holes in 1916, but scientists did not find one until 1971.

674. In the anime and manga series *Fullmetal Alchemist*, the suit-of-armor protagonist Alphonse Elric is typically referred to as Al, which is also the chemical symbol for aluminum.

675. Academic tenure is based on the idea that a permanent position promotes true academic freedom and is thus better for society at large.

676. Native Americans used cranberries for a variety of reasons, including food, dye, and medicine.

677. Pygmy is a term that generally refers to any ethnic group with a significantly shorter than

usual population. Historically, this has been associated with Central African communities.

678. Modern rolling suitcases, first called rollerboards, weren't invented until 1987.

679. The Przewalski's horse is the last known wild horse. They are found in Mongolia and central Asia.

680. Nathan Lane changed his first name from Joseph to Nathan based on the character Nathan Detroit from the musical *Guys and Dolls*. He is only 5 feet and 5 inches tall.

681. The late pop music artist Prince was baptized as a Jehovah's Witness in 2001.

682. In 2016, Germany and Sweden had the most powerful passports in the world. According to the Passport Index, each country is granted access to 158 different countries. A passport from Afghanistan, in comparison, has access to 24 countries.

683. Statelessness affects approximately 11 to 12 million people in the world, who have no birth certificate to prove their nationality or other crucial identifying information.

684. Bono, the lead singer of U2, got his nickname from the Latin word bonavox, translating as "good voice".

685. Jules Verne, author of *Around the World in 80 Days*, is credited as being one of the founders of the science fiction literature genre.

686. The average yurt can house 5 to 15 people.

687. Ancient Greco-Roman midwives often were regarded as highly as their male doctor peers for their knowledge and services.

688. The Official World Naked Bike Ride is a clothing-optional event which has been held in various cities every year since 2004.

689. Naomi Campbell appeared in Bob Marley's music video for "Is This Love" when she was 7 years old.

690. In the Thai language, the word 'thai' translates roughly as 'free man,' so the country of Thailand can be approximated as meaning 'free man land.'

691. Dandelion stems secrete latex when cut open, which when processed and refined can be a natural source of rubber.

692. Actor and environmental activist Leonardo DiCaprio owns an island off the coast of Belize called Blackadore Caye.

693. The original Teenage Mutant Ninja Turtles were cast as hitmen assigned to kill the character Shredder.

694. Narc is an abbreviation for both a narcotics officer and for a narcissist.

695. Krokodil, technically known as desomorphine, was a legal and patented form of medicine in the United States in the early 1930s. Krokodil as a recreational drug is known for being eight to ten times more powerful than morphine.

696. Bill Clinton was the second president in US history to be impeached. Andrew Johnson was the first to be impeached, in 1868.

697. In the television series *Community*, Sir Patrick Stewart was first considered for the character Pierce, but it ultimately went to Chevy Chase.

698. One of the alternate titles for Stanley Kubrick's film *2001: Space Odyssey* was *Journey Beyond the Stars*. This title appeared on the

official MGM press release in February 1965, but was soon changed by Kubrick.

699. Singer Alicia Keys married fellow recording artist Swizz Beatz in 2010.

700. Four of the most famous graduates of *The Mickey Mouse Club* are Britney Spears, Christina Aguilera, Ryan Gosling, and Justin Timberlake.

701. There is a robot named the Dressman which is designed and programmed to perfectly iron your clothes.

702. Playboy Magazine is available in Braille. Its first edition was in 1970.

703. The national flower of Wales is the daffodil.

704. The point where the countries of Jordan, Lebanon, Israel, and Syria all meet is called the Shouting Valley because of its echo properties.

705. The symbol on the current national Tunisian flag is inspired by the Ottoman flag, reflecting the country's history in the Ottoman Empire.

706. As a child, artist Frida Kahlo played a variety of sports as a method of rehabilitation from polio. Among them were swimming, boxing, wrestling, bicycling, and roller skating.

707. The Church of Scientology was banned by Wikipedia from editing any articles on their websites starting in 2009.

708. The tallest recorded football player in the NFL was Richard Sligh, who measured 7 feet tall and was a defensive tackle. The average height for running backs, in comparison, is 5 feet, 11 inches tall.

709. The quotation on the Liberty Bell comes from Leviticus 25:10.

710. The golden dollar coin featuring the Native American Sacagawea is not made of any actual gold. It is a copper core that is coated in manganese brass for a gold-like finish.

711. In Hindu culture, women typically have their nose pierced on the left side based on the believed connection between that part of the body and the female reproductive organs in Ayurveda medicine.

712. Eyebrows are crucial to successful facial recognition. The average eyebrow is made up of about 250 hairs.

713. Tom Cruise was a student at a Franciscan seminary as a teenager. He aspired to become a Catholic priest before realizing his acting career.

714. The first major label release by The Jackson 5 was affiliated with Diana Ross and the Supremes.

715. Retail giant Sears, Roebuck & Co is named after its two founders—Richard Warren Sears and Alvah Curtis Roebuck.

716. iRobot, the company behind the vacuuming robot Roomba, also manufactures a robot called the PackBot for the US Military, designed for stealth investigation.

717. Actress Blake Lively, born Blake Ellender Brown, was named after her grandmother's brother.

718. Aestheticians learning the technique of threading will often practice on pieces of velvet before practicing on human clients.

719. Fred Armisen and Carrie Bradshaw's on-screen dynamic in their show *Portlandia* is

inspired by *Sesame Street* characters Bert and Ernie.

720. The city of Austin, Texas, first coined the phrase "Keep Austin Weird" in 2003, which inspired other cities throughout the United States to do so as well, such as Portland, Oregon's, "Keep Portland Weird." Other cities include Louisville and Indianapolis.

721. The mansion featured in the first season of *American Horror Story: Murder House* has been used as the set for a variety of other television shows, including *Buffy the Vampire Slayer* and *Dexter*. It is known as the Rosenheim Mansion in real life and is a real home.

722. The famous murderer Ted Bundy both proposed to and married Carol Ann Boone during his trial while she was at the witness stand.

723. In his youth, Johnny Depp was a member of a garage band called The Kids, who opened for Iggy Pop in Los Angeles once before breaking up.

724. Lady Ching Shih was a notorious pirate in the early 19th century. She battled against British, Chinese, and Portuguese forces, and commanded thousands of vessels and crew members, but retired in 1810.

725. The Republic of Senegal is home to over 80 different political parties.

726. The process for knighthood in the Middle Ages was to become a page, then a squire, and finally a knight.

727. There are over 6,500 possible tangram configurations.

728. The shandy and the radler are both beers combined with juice or soda, except the shandy comes from Britain and the radler comes from Germany.

729. Convenience store chain 7-Eleven sells more than 100 million hot dogs every year.

730. White elephants are considered lucky in Burmese and Thai cultures.

731. A rabbit's foot charm is only considered effective if it is the left hind foot of the creature and if it was captured or killed in a

cemetery. Additionally, the phase of the moon, day of the week, and method of capture or killing may affect its legitimacy.

732. Crab shells are exoskeletons.

733. In America, sherbet and sorbet are not the same. Sherbet contains some dairy, while sorbet does not.

734. Senator John McCain graduated in the fifth lowest rank in his graduating class from The United States Naval Academy at Annapolis in 1958.

735. Lemons are historically a hybrid of the citron and the bitter orange.

736. Lisa Frank's iconic designs were first all drawn and colored by hand.

737. Both David Bowie and Elvis Presley had birthdays on January 8th.

738. Native American Pocahontas changed her name to Rebecca after marrying Englishman John Rolfe.

739. Chickenpox can be spread by physical contact as well as through the air.

740. Bongos are drums but are also a species of antelope found in central Africa.

741. In the vote for the Quebec referendum of 1995, in which the state sought to separate from Canada and establish itself as its own nation, the winning 'no' vote only surpassed the 'yes' votes by .16% of the total votes.

742. Harp seals nurse their newborn pups for 12 days before leaving them to fend for themselves in the wild.

743. There is a Tupperware party being held somewhere in the world approximately every 2 seconds.

744. Tom Monaghan, founder of pizza chain Domino's, met his wife when making a delivery to the dormitory building she worked in.

745. British law prohibits class A eggs, the kind found in supermarkets, from being washed or cleaned before being put on sale. The opposite applies in the United States.

746. The first reportedly successful human clones were created in 2002 and 2003, a girl and boy respectively, by the company CLONAID.

747. Iceland commonly refers to handball as being the national sport.

748. Horse physiology makes it impossible for them to vomit.

749. In Norway, the government buys 1,000 copies of any newly published book and distributes them to libraries throughout the country.

750. In the United States, 15 different states and the District of Columbia recognize Common Law Marriage, some with limitations.

751. The stevia plant, which can be used to create the sugar substitute by the same name, is a member of the sunflower family of plants.

752. Irish families have 1.4 children per household on average.

753. The Fighting Cholitas are an all-female group of female *lucha libres* in Bolivia. They wear the traditional Aymaran clothing during their matches, including tiered skirts and bowler hats.

754. The stone used in professional curling weighs between 38 to 44 pounds. Good sportsmanship is a core value of curling, and it is tradition for the winning team to buy a round of drinks and hot dogs for the losing team.

755. Character Harley Quinn's most notable abilities are her gymnastics skills, immunity to most poisons and toxins, and the ability to handle firearms.

756. The original story of the superhero Aquaman was written so that he was raised by dolphins.

757. China harvests and exports the majority of the world's garlic.

758. Vlad the Impaler, known as Vlad Dracula during his time, was a raider and leader in modern day Romania in the 1400s. His history was the inspiration for the character Count Dracula.

759. Human urine is made of approximately 95% water.

760. The technical term for when someone is aroused by vomit or watching someone else vomit is emetophilia.

761. Sylvia Plath's novel *The Bell Jar* was based on her real-life experiences with attempted suicide and subsequent residence in a mental hospital.

762. The appearance of large, guarded, centrally located cemeteries in the United States was the result of grave robbing and body snatching practices common in the 19th century.

763. Bounty hunting is illegal in Kentucky, Oregon, Illinois, and Wisconsin.

764. At the height of the Industrial Revolution, three-quarters of the workforce in the textile mills of Lowell, Massachusetts, were female.

765. Prairie dogs are a species of ground squirrels who received their misleading name because of their distinct barking sound.

766. In 1944, *The Daily Telegraph* published several crosswords with solutions containing the code names of top-secret D-Day operations. This became infamously known as the D-Day Daily Telegraph Crossword Security Alarm.

767. Despite its Japanese name, the game Sudoku was created in Europe. Sudoku itself is a trademarked game in Japan.

768. Anne Frank's father, Otto Frank, served in the Imperial German Army during World War I.

769. The first coloring books, published in the early 20th century, were meant to be painted rather than colored.

770. Public post boxes in Brazil are yellow.

771. There are over 10,000 man-made objects orbiting Earth.

772. Oysters are considered an aphrodisiac because they are rich in zinc, which is shown to affect progesterone.

773. It is generally an urban myth that eating more beans will increase flatulence.

774. Epsom salts are not actually salts one could eat, but are a chemical compound called magnesium sulfate made of magnesium, sulfur, and oxygen.

775. German inventor Karl Nessler invented both the permanent wave machine and the first false eyelashes.

776. The only moat built in Australia was built in Brisbane out of fear of Russian invasion around 1880. It is called Fort Lytton and is now a national park.

777. Shaman usually refers to a spiritual healer, but is more specifically referring to the Tungusic peoples of Siberia.

778. Dedicated Jimmy Buffett fans are often called parrotheads. Younger fans, or the children of parrotheads, are called parakeets.

779. The Bata Shoe Museum is the only one of its kind in North America dedicated to the history of shoes and other footwear. It is located in Toronto, Canada, and bears a coat of arms designed with a boot and two keys.

780. Labor Day was declared an official national holiday by former president Grover Cleveland.

781. Zulu is the name of both an ethnic group and the group's language. The Zulu people are the largest recorded ethnic group in South Africa.

782. The Ferris Wheel invented for the 1983 Chicago World's Fair was also used during the 1904 St. Louis World's Fair, otherwise known as the Louisiana Purchase Exposition.

783. Croxetti-cut pasta is a small, disc-like pasta stamped on both sides with detailed designs to resemble coat of arms or other unique patterns.

784. Rugby balls were initially made from, then later shaped after, pig bladders.

785. Miley Cyrus' godmother is country music legend Dolly Parton.

786. Anthrax can enter the body in four ways: through skin, lungs, digestion, and injection.

787. Tenacious D, the acoustic-metal duo of Jack Black and Kyle Gass, got its start from appearing in David Cross' television series *Mr. Show*.

788. Postpartum psychosis is the more severe development of postpartum depression, and is characterized by all the symptoms of depression as well a mental disengagement from reality.

789. Oktoberfest is rooted in the history and culture of Bavaria, which is a German state in the southeast region of the country.

790. Menarche is the technical term for the age when a girl begins to menstruate.

791. The PG-13 film rating was created by Steven Spielberg after controversy arose after the release of *Indiana Jones and The Temple of Doom*.

792. Staplers made before 1879 would insert the metal staple into the paper, but not fasten it. The fastening had to be done by-hand.

793. The ocarina is a real, flute-like instrument which dates back to over 12,000 years and was used in ancient Chinese and Mesopotamian cultures. The instrument was brought back to the public eye thanks to the video game *Legend of Zelda: Ocarina of Time*.

794. Country music artist Kenny Chesney's first guitar was named "The Terminator."

795. The three primary eating disorders are anorexia nervosa, bulimia nervosa, and binge eating disorder.

796. Billiard balls were primarily made with ivory until the early 20th century.

797. The parasite responsible for most swimming pool-water caused illnesses, cryptosporidium, is chlorine-tolerant.

798. The Pentagon building has no elevators.

799. The "MI" part of the British security organizations MI5 and MI6 stands for "Military Intelligence".

800. Many cruise ships are equipped with small on-board morgues in the event of passenger deaths.

801. The R.M.S. Titanic had its own official newspaper for guests, called the *Atlantic Daily Bulletin*.

802. Catalan is not a dialect of Spanish but rather a unique language with features similar to Italian, Portuguese, and Spanish.

803. Giraffes only need an average of 1.9 hours of sleep every day.

804. Moustache spoons were a popular piece of silverware with Victorian noblemen because

they were designed with a rim to guard their well-kept moustaches while eating.

805. In poultry, dark meat typically contains more zinc, iron, B12, B6, and riboflavin than white meat.

806. The first official Paralympic Games happened in Rome, Italy, in 1960.

807. Less-offensive alternatives to common profanities or curse words are called minced oaths.

808. Poet Maya Angelou created greeting cards with the company Hallmark Cards in 2000.

809. The first entrance examination produced by the College Board covered topics in Latin, French, English, German, Greek, History, Mathematics, Physics, and Chemistry.

810. When using a battery, typically electrons flow from the negative end to the positive end of the battery to create energy. When you re-charge that battery, the electrons flow in the opposite direction.

811. Emojis and wingdings are both classified as dingbat fonts.

812. Pho is typically eaten as a breakfast dish in its native Vietnam, but is eaten for lunch and dinner as well in foreign countries.

813. The classic children's book *The Very Hungry Caterpillar* is endorsed by the Royal Entomological Society.

814. When beloved children's book author Eric Carle was 15 years old, he was conscripted by the German army to dig trenches on the Siegfried line.

815. Sheriffs in the United States are elected into their role in their respective county.

816. The Dead Sea, due to its high salt content, cannot support any life forms in its waters other than some bacteria.

817. Buckingham Palace features 775 different rooms in its layout.

818. The garage in which the tech-company Hewlett Packard first started is now a historical landmark in the state of California.

819. Christian Bale almost was cast as Jack Dawson in the 1997 film *Titanic,* but lost it to Leonardo DiCaprio.

820. The Chessington World of Adventures, a zoo in the United Kingdom, prohibits its visitors from wearing animal prints on their property.

821. Raw shea butter can be used as a good substitute for butter, margarine, or lard.

822. The record for the fastest typing speed of American English is 375 words per minute (wpm).

823. The Patagonian Mara, a rodent resembling a deer and a rabbit, is found only in Argentina.

824. Chronologically, the order of Sophocles' Oedipus trilogy occurs as *Oedipus Rex, Oedipus at Colonus,* and finally *Antigone.*

825. Actor John Travolta appeared in the Broadway version of *Grease* before being cast in the film adaptation.

826. Black Nationalist Marcus Garvey was inspired by the beliefs of Zionism and later was influential in inspiring the Rastafari movement of the 1930s.

827. The most well-known Mormon temple is the Church of Jesus Christ of Latter-day Saints in Salt Lake City, Utah.

828. Blackberries are a natural source of vitamin K, which helps with muscle relaxation.

829. During the French Revolution, many tapestries were burnt or destroyed in order to extract the gold thread woven into their designs.

830. The boogeyman is a universal character who goes by several different names depending on the locale. In Germanic culture, it is the butzemann, while in Mediterranean cultures it is the babau.

831. The Los Angeles International Airport (LAX) incinerates all garbage collected from incoming international flights.

832. A crop circle is most likely a fake if the stalks and stems are broken and cannot be harvested anymore.

833. The two types of stone which make up Stonehenge are sarsen and bluestone.

834. Another name for the runic alphabets from Scandinavia is futhark.

835. On the planet Venus, the rain which falls consists of methane and sulfuric acid.

836. Jesters and troubadours eventually replaced minstrels as the primary form of entertainment in the European courts of the Middle Ages.

837. The five colors of traditional Tibetan prayer flags represent the five elements: space, air, fire, water, and earth.

838. The Star of David, also called the Shield of David, was a decorative symbol before it became associated with Judaism.

839. *Tao of Pooh* is a book which explains the core principles of Taoism, a classical Chinese philosophy and religion, through the narrative of Winnie the Pooh.

840. Confucianism was named the official imperial philosophy of the Chinese empire during the Han Dynasty.

841. The average chicken nugget contains almost 60 calories.

842. The Julian calendar was created by Julius Caesar shortly after the Roman conquest of Egypt and directly precedes the modern-day Gregorian calendar, created by Pope Gregory XIII in 1582.

843. The three main ideologies of the Black Panthers were socialism, black self-determination, and Marxism.

844. Haggis is both a sausage and a pudding.

845. The classic Australian condiment Vegemite is owned by an American company.

846. The first email ever sent was in 1971.

847. The State of Libya agreed to stop creating weapons of mass destruction in 2003.

848. Britney Spears was born in McComb, Mississippi.

849. The Republic of Côte d'Ivoire has two different capitals. Yamoussoukro is the country's political capital, while Abidjan is the economic capital.

850. Mature ivory is made of highly compressed dentine without enamel.

851. The original American cowboy hat was named "The Boss of The Plains" and was made by Stetson.

852. Voodoo is a religion that combines the beliefs and practices of various schools of thought and also has several regional variations with

their own unique practices, although they all have traditions rooted in African diaspora.

853. There were almost 1,500 Jewish delicatessens in New York City at the peak of their popularity. Only fifteen of those delis still exist.

854. Basketball icon Michael Jordan announced his first retirement from professional basketball in 1993 and pursued a professional baseball career under the Chicago White Sox. He returned to basketball in 1995.

855. Nunavut is the newest and least populous region of Canada, containing approximately 0.10% of the country's population. Their coat of arms features a moose and a narwhal.

856. The bestselling item in the commissary at the Rikers Island jail complex is instant noodles.

857. In 1999 Canada denied Greenpeace a non-profit organization status, despite the fact that the organization was formed by Canadians.

858. Volunteers in the Peace Corps have served in 141 countries since the program's inception in 1961.

859. Mountain Lake Lodge, the resort where several iconic scenes from the original *Dirty Dancing* were filmed, hosts three *Dirty Dancing*-themed getaway weekends annually.

860. Wireless Bluetooth technology was named after the 10th century Scandinavian king Harald Bluetooth. The Bluetooth logo is inspired by the runic alphabet.

861. Black Rock City is an LLC and only physically exists during the annual Burning Man music festival. The Black Rock Desert, for which it is named, is permanent.

862. The most populated station on the Bay Area Rapid Transit (BART) system is Embarcadero. The least populated is North Concord/ Martinez.

863. In the Portland, Oregon, metro area alone, there are 12 different bridges connecting the east and west sides of town.

864. Italic type is classified as a cursive font.

865. The male and female derivations of the term paparazzi are paparazzo and paparazza, respectively.

866. Although champagne and sparkling wine beverages are produced and sold throughout the world, only products made in the Champagne region of France can legally be labeled with the Champagne title.

867. Generally, whisky refers exclusively to the Scottish beverage, while whiskey refers to all variations of the spirit.

868. The average wooden telephone or utility pole can last between 40 to 60 years before needing to be replaced.

869. When you pop a pimple, the action creates a tear in the dermis layer which is then open to dirt and bacteria.

870. Blisters can be filled with plasma, serum, blood, or pus.

871. Normandy, France, is home to five different UNESCO World Heritage sites.

872. Japanese samurai warriors had a variety of swords which they used for specific purposes, but the katana is the most iconic of them. When paired with a smaller sword, the

combination was called a "daisho" and could only be worn by samurai.

873. The term potpourri comes from the French "pot-pourri," which roughly translates as "rotten pot."

874. The patchouli plant is native to Asian islands and was historically used as an insect repellant, especially against moths.

875. When moving a corpse, compressed air which has been trapped in the lungs and stomach can escape the body, resulting in a moan-like noise.

876. The early clothes hangers created by men's clothier Meyer May in 1906 were inspired by the shape of a wishbone.

877. Saint Catherine's Monastery is home to the world's oldest continuously operating library, although the library itself is not open to the public.

878. Fashion consultant Tim Gunn was not paid for his first two seasons working on *Project Runway*. He also identifies as asexual.

879. Norilsk is the northernmost city in the world and is located in the Arctic Circle in

Krasnoyarsk Krai, Russia. The city flag features a bear holding a key overhead.

880. The location of the Arctic Circle on the Earth shifts north approximately 15 meters per year.

881. The state of Georgia produces the most pecans in the United States.

882. The Florida Keys seceded from the United States in 1982 and declared itself the Conch Republic.

883. The first episodes of Steve Irwin's nature television show *The Crocodile Hunter* consisted of crocodile trapping video footage shot during his honeymoon with Terri Raines.

884. Maggie Gyllenhaal's first name is short for Margalit.

885. The original *Match Game* game show series would film all of its season's episodes over the course of one weekend.

886. Actress Betty White has been married three separate times.

887. The traditional method of drinking yerba mate is in a hollow gourd and through a *bombilla*, a metal straw with a built-in filter.

888. The alternate spelling for bagel is biegel.

889. The Spam Museum, which celebrates the ubiquitous pork product, is located in Austin, Minnesota.

890. Darth Vader was played by three separate actors during the filming of the original trilogy. David Prowse was the body actor, James Earl Jones was the voice actor, and Sebastian Shaw was the "face" actor.

891. Napalm is made from gasoline, polystyrene, and benzene.

892. The Vietnam War resulted in approximately 1 million civilian deaths.

893. Ronald Wilson Reagan appeared in 53 films during his acting career before he became president of the United States.

894. The classic Mary Jane style of shoe was considered a unisex style until the 1930s, when it became associated with women's and girl's fashion.

895. Moccasins are traditionally made out of deerskin.

896. Pumpkin carving was initially an Irish tradition.

897. The first razors were fashioned in copper and date back to approximately 3000 BCE.

898. Singles Awareness Day is the alternative holiday to Valentine's Day. Its acronym is, appropriately, SAD.

899. St. Patrick's Day, as a religious holiday, celebrates the introduction of Christianity to Ireland.

900. April Fools' Day is not a recognized public holiday in any country in the world. Both the pranks and their victims which happen this day are referred to as April Fools.

901. The first commercially sold skateboards had wheels made of clay. The modern polyurethane wheels were not created until the 1970s.

902. In South America, red sweet potatoes are used to create cloth dye.

903. Actress Mindy Kaling's television series *The Mindy Project* was initially titled *It's Messy*.

904. Athens, Georgia, is home to famous musical groups the B-52's and REM.

905. Vegetable glue, despite its name, is any glue made from plants.

906. North and South Dakota are named after the Dakota tribe which resided in that region. In the Sioux language, Dakota translates approximately as "friend."

907. Buffalo Bill began working for the Pony Express, a mail service which connected the American Midwest to the West coast during the mid-1800s, when he was 14 years old.

908. Chief Sitting Bull nicknamed the famous sharp-shooter Annie Oakley *Watanya Cicillia*, which translates as "Little Sure Shot" in English.

909. Oceania as a region is comprised of 25 nations.

910. The Waffle Index is an informal metric for determining the severity and damage of a natural disaster.

911. There are four classifications of drought: meteorological, agricultural, hydrological, and socioeconomic.

912. Legendary rock group Led Zeppelin made several candid references to J.R.R. Tolkien's *The Lord of the Rings* trilogy in their lyrics and song titles.

913. The Zeppelin was a German invention but was patented in the United States in 1899. They were then used by the German Army in World War I.

914. The peak season for tangerines is approximately November through January.

915. NASCAR is short for the National Association for Stock Car Auto Racing.

916. It is a tradition at the Indianapolis "Indy" 500 for the winner of the race to drink a bottle of milk. Their options are skim, whole, and 2% milk.

917. The official drink of the Kentucky Derby is the mint julep, made specifically with Kentucky bourbon.

918. Japanese tabi socks are the earliest precursors of modern day toe socks.

919. Roof tiles which are flat are commonly used in Southern Germany and are known as "beaver tail" tiles because of their shape.

920. The Alaskan Malamute is a purebred dog and one of the oldest of Alaska's native sled dogs. The Alaskan Husky, in comparison, is a mixed breed who was bred exclusively for working and is not recognized by the American Kennel Club.

921. The United Nations began with 51 countries and currently consists of 193.

922. The calorie value associated with a food item measures that item's specific food energy.

923. The original model for the now common 3.5 mm phone connector design was first conceived in the late 19th century and gradually became smaller and more compact with the advancement of technology,

924. Cotton candy was invented by dentists at the turn of the 20th century. It was called "fairy floss" and was debuted at the St. Louis World's Fair in 1904.

925. Canadian recording artist Justin Bieber's mentor is actor Will Smith.

926. The mechanical noise roller coaster cars make when ascending a peak is a safety mechanism called the anti-rollback device.

927. The world-famous Astronomical clock in Prague signals every hour with a procession of 12 apostles, ending with death.

928. To qualify for the United States Navy SEAL program, applicants must be able to complete a minimum of 42 pushups in 2 minutes. The optimum number is 100 in 2 minutes.

929. The order of fragrances based on oil concentration and scent intensity, from most to least, is Eau de Parfum, Eau de Toilette, and Eau de Cologne.

930. The trademark of any Johnny Rockets diner franchise is receiving a smiley face made out of ketchup on a paper plate with an order of fries.

931. Otter feces are technically known as spraint.

932. Tennessee has the strictest laws against lock picking in the United States.

933. Cricket fields were commonly encircled by picket fences until the 1980s.

934. In the Narragansett Bay area of Massachusetts, the see-saw is colloquially known as a dandle or dandle board.

935. Cat burglars are named as such due to their ability to scale walls to enter homes through upstairs windows and stealthily walk across roofs and other tricky terrain.

936. L'esprit de l'escalier is an expression coined by the French philosopher Denis Diderot.

937. The sensitive period during which a child is capable of acquiring any language lasts approximately from birth to six months of age.

938. The International Butler Academy, located in the Netherlands, offers comprehensive, 8-week intensive programs on the art of being a professional butler.

939. Historically, the best man of the groom was whomever he chose to help capture his wife-to-be, as well as the person who would prevent the woman from running away or being reclaimed by her family.

940. The Oneida colony located in New York State in the mid-19th century practiced complex marriage, a form of polyamory or group marriage.

941. Despite destroying the majority of the city, the Great Fire of London only claimed approximately sixteen lives.

942. The classic nursery rhyme "Mary, Mary, Quite Contrary" is about Queen Mary I of England's violent execution of Protestants under her rule. Her nickname was Bloody Mary.

943. The median age of the population of Yemen is 18.9 years old.

944. The Day of the Goose is a competition held during the San Antolin festival in Basque Country and celebrates the hard work and endurance of the Basque population. In this event a grease-covered goose is hung beneath the harbor head-down, and young men jump from their boats to try and remove the head.

945. The World Nomad Games celebrates the nomadic cultures and traditions of Central

Asian communities and includes games such as eagle hunting and kok-boru.

946. In the children's television series *Blue's Clues,* the human main character Steve was initially envisioned as being female, while the cartoon puppy Blue had been first drawn as an orange cat.

947. Wine decanters serve two purposes; they filter sediment out of older wines and aerate the wine to allow oxygen to help fully release its flavors.

948. The earliest compasses, invented by the Chinese, were used as divination tools. They began to be used as navigation tools around the 11th century, also by the Chinese.

949. Nutmeg spice comes from the seeds of its trees and is not actually a nut product.

950. In Amsterdam, there are more bicycles than there are people living in the city.

951. Approximately 99.4% of all retailers continue to advertise through newspapers.

952. Coal ash is used as a filler for tennis rackets and golf balls.

953. Standard dragon boats require 22 bodies to operate; 20 paddlers, 1 caller, and 1 steerer.

954. Open-air funeral pyres are traditional in the Hindu and Sikh religions and are still widely practiced.

955. In badminton, the shuttlecock or birdie is made with 16 feathers.

956. A person's zodiac sign is determined based on the position of the sun at the time of birth.

957. Hailstones form in the clouds of thunderstorms and only fall once they become too heavy to be supported by the updraft.

958. Sandalwood oil is often used in fluorescence microscopy, as well as in aromatherapy.

959. The lifespan of a gladiator in ancient Rome typically lasted until their mid-20s.

960. Incense made with citronella materials can be used as effective natural insect repellents.

961. Although the Trojan Horse is a legend from the ancient Greek and Roman texts recounting the Sack of Troy, it is also now a metaphor for deceit or trickery.

962. Vince Vaughn shares the same initials with his two sisters, named Victoria and Valeri.

963. The Myers-Briggs Type Indicator personality test was inspired by the works of Carl Jung.

964. Humans lose 1 to 5 eyelashes daily.

965. World-famous soccer player Cristiano Ronaldo's full name is Cristiano Ronaldo dos Santos Aveiro. He was named "Ronaldo" after Ronald Reagan.

966. Actor Jamie Dornan was the face for Dior Homme in the 2007 ad campaign.

967. Rush Limbaugh is the third member of his immediate family to bear that exact name.

968. Hip-hop group N.W.A. preferred to be classified as "reality rap" rather than "gangsta rap" despite the explicit content of their lyrics.

969. Fairy bread is a treat consisting of buttered white bread topped with sprinkles. It is popular for children's parties in Australia and New Zealand.

970. In 2014, the animal rights group PETA reported euthanizing 81% of the animals which ended-up in its shelters.

971. Grilled cheese was not commonly made as a sandwich until the 1960s. Before that, it was typically prepared open-face style, with only one piece of bread.

972. Approximately half of the Trader Joe's grocery stores in existence are located in California State.

973. Figs are a member of the mulberry family of flowering plants.

974. Approximately 1.6 to 2.8 billion youths run away from home every year.

975. When lizards self-amputate their tails, the regrown tail will typically be a different color and texture than the rest of the body.

976. Birds, turtles, and crocodiles are all classified as reptiles.

977. Komodo Dragon females can successfully reproduce without sperm because of parthenogenesis.

978. The modern Union Jack flag embodies and blends together the design elements of three older national flags: Britain, Scotland, and Ireland.

979. Drew and Jonathan Scott, the brothers who host HGTV's popular television show *Property Brothers*, have a third sibling named J.D. who has had his own successful career in the entertainment industry.

980. The four Commonwealth states in the United States are Massachusetts, Kentucky, Pennsylvania, and Virginia.

981. Londinium was the first incarnation of the modern city of London. It was formed by the Romans in 47 AD as a trading post.

982. While Adolf Hitler was serving in the German army during World War I in 1918, a gas attack during battle left him temporarily blind.

983. Grandfather clocks received their name after the song *My Grandfather's Clock* which referenced the longcase clock.

984. Comedian Demetri Martin studied law before pursuing comedy. His younger brother's name is Spyro.

985. Bok choy is a subspecies of turnip and belongs to the same genus as cauliflower.

986. The average walrus pregnancy period lasts 15 to 16 months.

987. Conservative radio and television personality Sean Hannity won NAB Marconi Radio Awards for his program *The Sean Hannity Show* in 2003 and 2007.

988. The 20th century film star Charlie Chaplin was banned from re-entering the United States in 1952 because of his political and moral views.

989. A volleyball player will jump approximately 300 times in a typical match.

990. Edward Snowden broke both of his legs during an accident while training to become a soldier for the US Army Reserves.

991. Pinball was banned throughout the United States, and especially in New York City, starting in the 1940s and lasting until 1976.

992. Alternative names for the pasta found in alphabet soup is Alfabeto or Alphagetti.

993. The Asia Pacific Harmonica Festival is one of the largest harmonica gatherings in the world.

It has been held every two years in various locations throughout Asia since 1996.

994. The WikiLeaks Party is a micro political party formed in 2013 and based in Australia. The Party was deregistered in 2015.

995. The famous magician and escape artist Harry Houdini's younger brother, who went by the stage name Hardeen, also had a very successful career in magic. The brothers often performed together throughout the beginning of the 20th century and pretended to be rivals to boost attendance.

996. The name of the iconic photography company Kodak was chosen because it means nothing by itself and is hard to mispronounce.

997. Hair braiding has historically been a method of socializing and passing on community traditions through generations of family members, especially in African cultures.

998. Educator Helen Keller lost both her ability to see and hear when she was only 19 months old as a complication of an illness.

999. The planet Uranus is named after the Greek god Oranus, god of the sky, father of Cronus and grandfather of Zeus.

1000. The slang military term for the distance of one kilometer is a "klick."

More Books by Bill O'Neill

THE BIG BOOK OF
RANDOM
FACTS

BILL O'NEILL

Please,

If you liked this book, leave a review on Amazon. It helps me a lot! Make sure you check out the rest of my books on Amazon.

Until next time,
Bill O'Neill